pleasure is a miracle
Bianca Rae Messinger

pleasureis amiracle
Bianca Rae Messinger

Nightboat Books
New York

ISBN: 978-1-64362-241-5

Design and typesetting by Rissa Hochberger
Typeset in Neue Haas Grotesk

Cover art: "Design for a book illustration:
the effect of bombs falling on a town" by
Charles-Nicolas Cochin fils, graphite on
vellum, 1740. Collection of the Waddesdon
(National Trust), UK.

Cataloging-in-publication data is available
from the Library of Congress

Nightboat Books
New York
www.nightboat.org

contents

L. *Happy.* 'Tis true, but not from pleasures; for, I intend to incloister my self from the World, to enjoy pleasure, and not to bury my self from it; but to incloister my self from the incumbred cares and vexations, troubles and perturbance of the World.

M. CAVENDISH,
THE CONVENT OF PLEASURE

Very due that being each one dwells
through errant woods of stone
and roaming unknown streams
where few prints mark the air
contested only by that dare
and the narrow path
bending
but
to
where

N. H. PRITCHARD,
"THE NARROW PATH"

prelude: how painful was that place for her

here you and i were thieves, *always having to go somewhere*
for the night, and it being already a surprise in memory, and in
its immediacy which you called "following the rules," for instance
leaving in the middle of a hurricane—in 3 plays we're supposed to
be convinced and in its following we allow the use of slowing, it
being what you wanted and me instead trying to mirror things on
the television while we're lost in the age of reason.

i hope you're right, not about discipline but about divisions,
about it being a specific kind of knowledge, but i'd feel better
if it were related to some repetitive action, not as its same but
something you could put in a biography, not belonging to a
particular set, or even something anyone would have to read, and
not as a representation—but instead to have the ability tell when
something adds movement.

pleasureis

he approached, perceiving the remains of an abbey which stood on a rude lawn by high spreading trees, him not being coeval with the building but trying and a greater part of the pile sinking having withstood us shewing the remaining features of the fabric and our living in it and began:

I.

Dear Joanna – it has been
snowing, now, i take your car
to thepost office – on our small
walk i think your tape where
youmention space plays – OK *also because time is*
itplays again   *death*

i wanted to say "thank you" i guess i become interested in pleasure – in how you are a very distinct   pleasure because you have no time. it seems to be moving only slightly or you have tosort out that it is OK.

like a memory away

there's a fire on the first floor
or it smells like one. OK, here's
a good one – & with you it's *unless it's a repository*
not exceedingly difficult totrust *in public*
i mean it's easy – we also
don't have much of a choice.
because touse this *moving* feels
so timeless when outside is so
tragic:

response, is when isee what
iwant tosee of you in your
window, not on "the notes side of
things"– in that there, wehave an   *of debt.*
inability to see where *that* leads
an eventual falling over–being
OK with *that* & putting more
than what you have into it
i.e. a production.

next scene, this is called its happening over an eventual. youcall that choice but it's not, OK—it's like putting up sails–but as a circle, this eventual evening. it feels like a you from elsewhere (not inside)

so windowful

wefight in your red car over space,
whether it's consecutive, you say   *whether it's observatory*
no,   i say no too as i tend toagree
without wantingto, but yet   each
moment feels improvisatory when –
we're with our   main   OK – when
we're   with you

II.

Weresolve the argument with a narrative. on the deck everyone has a pussy but you. in dusk you show people   at the   party this come between their legs this wisteria, *and them putting* dripping overarching what was your *it inside of me* house. then people start fucking– start showing each other their pussies they're like these beams oflight that come between their legs & envelopeus but not because of entering but because they come down to us.

it happening over the rosewood, which is attached to what is your house, and its golden porch. in this next scene, it remains that we're beyond vis a vis "the world," *an endless* meaning it accommodates itself *postponement of* verywell toits being a charm, or *its same* girth, the sheer size of the fucking, youtry putting it in. in response you become attached toparadise–

Like those whosay light accumulates – step closer understanding that weshudder at what youbuild. you looks out a window, gray field, gray (light), in anattempt tocompromise between them. and it all notso much fucking as adistance as it is space uncharting

its main characteristic wasits unattainability

but it's stilloccurring as a question
and your answer to it – in thinking
of that room in particular, not as
an order, sowing a particular
thinking, called "in thinking of
you." in thinking of you, i think
through a passage or   a narrow
path of that room ithink, of a
narrow path and not a woman at
the end of it thereis no before only
in thinking of that room in thinking
of you in thinking of you I think of
that room in monterey i'm in the
room in monterey in having been
fucking in the hotel monterey
in thinking of you always in that
room in monterey with curtains
so in thinking of a room that
room in the hotel monterey in
monterey with curtains i think
of you in monterey in thinking
of you of me lying on the bed
of that room in hotel monterey
i think of you in between blue
and orange in thinking of the
cures for chronophobia i think
of you in that room of that room
in monterey calling into question
the   entire   operation – i   lose
that you, as you get too close
in thinking of you in that room
in monterey in thinking of you in
blue but not because you   are,
but you are in monterey aren't
you?

exactly

as it happens between blue and *in the rationalistic*
orange now again or tiled as from *shadowland*
before its beginning – then again
it happens but only in thinking –
but in monterey in thinking of you
as it happens in the bluedoor
and using it to dispel the pains
of chronic chronophobia – her
sitting there, and it not being
an action and thinking in that
room   and its narrow path
and its curtains. you would
remember it that way.

that room in thinking as it
moves – as a fallout shelter
and as a woman in thinking
but not before – if only to cure   *instead, having a*
the pains of chronophobia in   *knowledge   of*
monterey with her cunt in a   *elsewhere*
hotel room in caution. speaking
of you, goto the telephone, call
monterey call other time with
curtains in thinking of you call
me in the hotel monterey as it is
achieved through curtains and
a narrow path and an elevator
is how it is achieved only now
the door closing in the hotel in
monterey as it were as where
there is fucking – only ithink
in nylon curtains this room
not having sweep in it. then,
out in the loose weather –
him in the flooded warehouse
patrolling, her lying with the
drywall andhim covering her in
the dust of it going inside her
and the deepening of it.

III.

as for we who love to be
undone – becoming rope or
some tiny elevator resembling
its cover being exactly in
packing sheets– sothat
youwould not recognize the
object gesturing ormoving
upwards to you – you wander
through some series of
images, of tracks in rows
"trains," remembering slowly
how everything is ordered.   *so it's me*
& us two being carried &   *there*
its reeling, not falling but
going upward i remember
it different now – not having
escaped but rather going up

no back movement a severing as you move to the side, you say, "yes, this is aterminal, a body of play. not a yard." as we said before, structures always wait for some folding, or someone says it and there's a rising action or a soft wave that goes over, not a streak. it's about free time, some people *though it feels like a very long* call it newtime. kinds of *time ago* waiting go on forever. i call that fading.

now put more movement into it, it grounds well, she walks behind plexiglass the play opens she falls out of her cunt. see, we come out of the shaft first into the top of the building, and we have to wait there for a while, still seated, for the space w h e r e — s o m e t i m e s when we're quiet, the snow has anerotic value, a proscenium almost rises over us (out of its original between position) not now but another time, where we don't have to come out of her.

"oh, no, yes that's an overture"

having experienced this –
a form ofposing – no control
"exactly" but aplace where
everyone looks at their
manners fromoutside, there's
anassembly. you sound angry *she says she watches me*
(to you). now she talks ofwork, *sleep.*
& where she puts it. but yes,
in any erotic system which
deflnes the good, youcarry a
brick towards where it needs
to go, and when a task in
knowledge is imaginary
whileinthe scene it shifts to
orange – taking her pussy out
rightthere – there is daylight –
& brackets.

V.

how young wewere for those
counter   arguments – like
looking for asecond without
feeling disparate. itis that we
do it differently when wetalk
about   ourselves – last   night
over dinner we discover that
ourroad is broken but more
where youare last night with
her wherewe're on a train with
ourfather and thinking about the
stations and being leftwanting
or   what   works   like   that?
itseems like you have toget
there at a withouttime – we ask
him. we walk underground and
there's this pyramidal pavilion
wehave   little   walking   sticks
and it's like when we took the
train togoback inside but in the
dream it rained –

*proper routing
procedures*

24

whatyou miss is beauty, we say
to her, when it moves so quickly
and being attached – to be
attached instead of moving
around it, feeling what's to feel
over a continuum instead of a
sharp peakandvalley, and il's
not thatit's formal but instead
feels like an invitation – there is
acreation of an expanse, which
is not acounter argument we
had *cinq à sept* in a landlord's
garden. no one gets evicted.

CODA, or the world that they lost

june 21st 7:17pm

and cataract, for example, i had to give up my sense of it for the shallow conveyor of snow, we have milk in the fridge now, from before we discovered the sublime. i was afraid of it, in there being no speed to it. my numbers do not field back to memory.

and scaffolded, telling it as a view then things being smaller in reality, and the bugs on the grass, in clumps. the man with the grey shirt goes on standing in — somehow there's you in the well of footsteps, better "than anything"

and not now, earlier, falling into the rosicrucian mode. making
clippings of things made me feel stupider and stupider – a
man walks into the elevator, she looked down at her pussy. i
make a depiction to create tension, she said, with the sound
of green fringe

and roses where she walked, so an assertion. beneath an
enervated lake, I could feel it expanding then, orange walls, how
one tries to resuscitate interest. you can take it like a team, he
says – we walked by cones and it was an impossible ending. me
surrounded by self-sabotage, your camera and yours

and i, reach out in a way that can only be described as avoidance, as the soft puddles come up from the ground, it seems, it being set to a kind of perverse functionality. then again, there were those, the ones who did know what happened, and that being a different kind of thing

every bathroom full like a show

I.

that morning will feel quite luminous
where it's visible not necessarily but where
it's possible to be so — then what will
we do tomorrow — is there any imperious
sight for you now — greying in the corner, then
that's what you did at old cafés when time was
less valuable — not against sadness exactly
or still vacant but not without character
still moving at times problems of moving
not to worry then about softness returning
don't hurry it or keep our time whole on that
corner a table & a child comes up & around
barely visible then slips away — not gone
just out of the frame — then moving.
then morning morning comes & you start
licking me working down towards a now
here you are on a curb that matches the
street with no disambiguation – she rides
an elephant banging on cymbals – give
more palliative licks – last session – but
what will *we* do

II.

in moving faster than what we hereby certify
you seem to find some photograph you'd
forgotten the front matter, meaning not exactly
able to feel it – and yet one could call it happiness
but rather fall into morning – cat outside now walking on grass
as if moving beneath her at the same time – gliding
and what else is there – yellow white and purple
whose flag is that? must be someone's – when is it over
it's not low water it's just the opposite – but no
mention of it.

III.

my final note regarding some actions
doing everything   at once doesn't
feel like doing anything doesn't feel like
an action exactly a stroller passing by
the window   two cops slinking by stupidly
check the mail there's nothing there just
that's the story you'll tell that's what it's like to
watch the walls "as much as" the rain
try to flatten yourself try to listen to yourself
maybe a couple – people like that – that
gleaming again on the far side of the
roof, to the right, to my right. this neighborhood
smells like the one I grew up in but
that's 300 miles away

I'm sorry I haven't called
you you must be well — well
my mother says so, do I
trust her do I trust you — not
three not flies more
nasturtiums more y'know lilacs
heavy birds "hey bird I
want to be you."

it being unrelenting

a leg on the beach covered in sun because of all the fires
you hear between it then around sometimes and us two
or the three of us create a collaborative postcard which
becomes 3 postcards with the number 5 on all of them
being the set. then in the dull substance of my injurious
reason I realize why and there's a clicking in the back
ground. having trouble, so I must attend time's leisure and I
moan, and so you're here – in the corner with your eyes
    closed. hey,
this part could be seen as sulking or remembering, or coming
those moments that could be "forever," it's only fair, each some
thing means something to somebody. in the distance a man shouting,
"hey moneybags!" then stealing a car and getting away with it.
distance should come despite of space upon the farthest earth
thought kills me, then you forget that you can't see time before you,
it being a spaceship. [a la winded] distance should come
    despite of space
upon the farthest earth. then some men come down the
    backyard – thought
kills me, when you forget that you can't see time before you.
remember when you still had some desire to see objects,
i don't know, do you think this could be a feature, a feature of both
the thing and its consequences? here's one, a consequence here,
in watching a woman run into the lake her being on fire – then three
trees scratch the windows, commissioning it like a railway at the
heart of it a crypt – the carts sliding past these men, then being
poked through by gorgeous fingernails. surrounded by a moat the sky
goes low but we don't fuck anyone in this movie, being
resolute, then her grabbing me by the throat.

then there being a field of rhododendrons, you use them as
bait that I hold in a way how you make a necklace, it rides up
my neck. you having a real fear of equanimity. just "walking up to
it and feeling before" — how long is the waking up? for the
point of moving was where it came from, being how my
impetus becomes a part of your world, tying the flowers
to the bottom of the river. my sister comes back to life but
isn't this the way you'd want it? everything starts in vibration
at some point — maybe like a moment of emergence, my
paper my little paper. working on my promises. thanks. you
stand in front of a room and i don't need to tell them your
power. everything that happens to me in this is because
of her. it being dark but the sky still having cohesion.

ravishing of a field

A spiral is the shape of a progression of circles. Thus myopia may serve to dispel the pains of chronophobia.

& then in that gray field some smallness

becomes focus. becomes 2 men in

yellow vests. it resembles little

but feels this conflagration.

because a balance is created but

not in

representation.

so that memory looks like what it feels,

not that exact signaling, but some
formation without regret

to get to a point where it is not
returning but

recombining – which is what it is. not a
progression.

maybe being myopic is being what
the shape of a lamp

feels like or the timbre of a sunset

or the crease in a back as you slide

your arm across it

time so that it includes –

wondering how ayou connects
onwards –

needing to touch a fountain in paris &
never having been and needing it to

happen quickly. but you were always
more

wary than me, except by what was
necessary

slow & profound as it makes
anecho.

this space being so massive from the
mountains on every side

afraid, so smoking. "so much space

to be filled" being what they say

is value in an idea – a last visit before

it's just getting out with itself. visit
before

she's gone isn't it, I will wake up
there wont i –

then, looking attheir own
space dotted

crossed like. more that she
wanted

me being a habit of it, inits
neighbor

and in the time ofher
thinking it, of a roundabout,

of wantingtocome needing
it, actually

and for once being able to
get that across. coming and
the marking

she makes on your leg of its
making. what –

at that point time felt small, a
step lighteras she looks

to the source of its
movement:

which we call:

beginning

then the mail comes as
arecording, o fits of intimacy

eachred strand trapped in
an orange

tube, & it wasn't todo with
her instead they call it
gratification –

fearing control but wantingit
deeply

& unattachable
simultaneously

which surprised me,

looming against

progresssssssssssssssssssssssssssssssssssssssssssssss
ssssssssssssssssssssssssssssssssssssssssssssssssssssss
ssssssssssssssssssssssssssssssssssssssssssssssssssssss
ssssssssssssssssssssssssssssssssssssssssssssssssssssss
ssssssssssssssssssssssssssssssssssssssssssssssssssssss
ssssssssssssssssssssssssssssssssssssssssssssssssssssss
ssssssssssssssssssssssssssssssssssssssssssssssssssssss
ssssssssssssssssssssssssssssssssssssssssssssssssssssss
ssssssssssssssssssssssssssssssssssssssssssssssssssssss
ssssssssssssssssssssssssssssssssssssssssssssssssssssss
ssssssssssssssssssssssssssssssssssssssssssssssssssssss
ssssssssssssssssssssssssssssssssssssssssssssssssssssss
ssssssssssssssssssssssssssssssssssssssssssssssssssssss
ssssssssssssssssssssssssssssssssssssssssssssssssssssss
ssssssssssssssssssssssssssssssssssssssssssssssssssssss
ssssssssssssssssssssssssssssssssssssssssssssssssssssss
ssssssssssssssssssssssssssssssssssssssssssssssssssssss
ssssssssssssssssssssssssssssssssssssssssssssssssssssss
ssssssssssssssssssssssssssssssssssssssssssssssssssssss
ssssssssssssssssssssssssssssssssssssssssssssssssssssss
ssssssssssssssssssssssssssssssssssssssssssssssssssssss
ssssssssssssssssssssssssssssssssssssssssssssssssssssss
ssssssssssssssssssssssssssssssssssssssssssssssssssssss
ssssssssssssssssssssssssssssssssssssssssssssssssssssss-
ssssssssssssssssssssssssssssssssssssssssssssssssssssss

SSSSSSSSSSSSSSSSSSSSSSSSSSSSSSSSSSSSSSSSSSSSSSSSSSS
SSSSSSSSSSSSSSSSSSSSSSSSSSSSSSSSSSSSSSSSSSSSSSSSSSS
SSSSSSSSSSSSSSSSSSSSSSSSSSSSSSSSSSSSSSSSSSSSSSSSSSS
SSSSSSSSSSSSSSSSSSSSSSSSSSSSSSSSSSSSSSSSSSSSSSSSSSS
SSSSSSSSSSSSSSSSSSSSSSSSSSSSSSSSSSSSSSSSSSSSSSSSSSS
SSSSSSSSSSSSSSSSSSSSSSSSSSSSSSSSSSSSSSSSSSSSSSSSSSS
SSSSSSSSSSSSSSSSSSSSSSSSSSSSSSSSSSSSSSSSSSSSSSSSSSS
SSSSSSSSSSSSSSSSSSSSSSSSSSSSSSSSSSSSSSSSSSSSSSSSSSS
SSSSSSSSSSSSSSSSSSSSSSSSSSSSSSSSSSSSSSSSSSSSSSSSSSS
SSSSSSSSSSSSSSSSSSSSSSSSSSSSSSSSSSSSSSSSSSSSSSSSSSS
SSSSSSSSSSSSSSSSSSSSSSSSSSSSSSSSSSSSSSSSSSSSSSSSSSS
SSSSSSSSSSSSSSSSSSSSSSSSSSSSSSSSSSSSSSSSSSSSSSSSSSS
SSSSSSSSSSSSSSSSSSSSSSSSSSSSSSSSSSSSSSSSSSSSSSSSSSS
SSSSSSSSSSSSSSSSSSSSSSSSSSSSSSSSSSSSSSSSSSSSSSSSSSS
SSSSSSSSSSSSSSSSSSSSSSSSSSSSSSSSSSSSSSSSSSSSSSSSSSS
SSSSSSSSSSSSSSSSSSSSSSSSSSSSSSSSSSSSSSSSSSSSSSSSSSS
SSSSSSSSSSSSSSSSSSSSSSSSSSSSSSSSSSSSSSSSSSSSSSSSSSS
SSSSSSSSSSSSSSSSSSSSSSSSSSSSSSSSSSSSSSSSSSSSSSSSSSS
SSSSSSSSSSSSSSSSSSSSSSSSSSSSSSSSSSSSSSSSSSSSSSSSSSS
SSSSSSSSSSSSSSSSSSSSSSSSSSSSSSSSSSSSSSSSSSSSSSSSSSS
SSSSSSSSSSSSSSSSSSSSSSSSSSSSSSSSSSSSSSSSSSSSSSSSSSS
SSSSSSSSSSSSSSSSSSSSSSSSSSSSSSSSSSSSSSSSSSSSSSSSSS
SSSSSSSSSSSSSSSSSSSSSSSSSSSSSSSSSSSSSSSSSSSSSSSSSSS
SSSSSSSSSSSSSSSSSSSSSSSSSSSSSSSSSSSSSSSSSSSSSSSSSSS
SSSSSSSSSSSSSSSSSSSSSSSSSSSSSSSSSSSSSSSSSSSSSSSSSSS
SSSSSSSSSSSSSSSSSSSSSSSSSSSSSSSSSSSSSSSSSSSSSSSSSSS
SSSSSSSSSSSSSSSSSSSSSSSSSSSSSSSSSSSSSSSSSSSSSSSSSSS
SSSSSSSSSSSSSSSSSSSSSSSSSSSSSSSSSSSSSSSSSSSSSSSSSSS
SSSSSSSSSSSSSSSSSSSSSSSSSSSSSSSSSSSSSSSSSSSSSSSSSSS
SSSSSSSSSSSSSSSSSSSSSSSSSSSSSSSSSSSSSSSSSSSSSSSSSSS
SSSSSSSSSSSSSSSSSSSSSSSSSSSSSSSSSSSSSSSSSSSSSSSSSSS
SSSSSSSSSSSSSSSSSSSSSSSSSSSSSSSSSSSSSSSSSSSSSSSSSSS
SSSSSSSSSSSSSSSSSSSSSSSSSSSSSSSSSSSSSSSSSSSSSSSSSSS
SSSSSSSSSSSSSSSSSSSSSSSSSSSSSSSSSSSSSSSSSSSSSSSSSSS
SSSSSSSSSSSSSSSSSSSSSSSSSSSSSSSSSSSSSSSSSSSSSSSSSSS
SSSSSSSSSSSSSSSSSSSSSSSSSSSSSSSSSSSSSSSSSSSSSSSSSSS
SSSSSSSSSSSSSSSSSSSSSSSSSSSSSSSSSSSSSSSSSSSSSSSSSSS
SSSSSSSSSSSSSSSSSSSSSSSSSSSSSSSSSSSSSSSSSSSSSSSSSSS
SSSSSSSSSSSSSSSSSSSSSSSSSSSSSSSSSSSSSSSSSSSSSSSSSSS

```
SSSSSSSSSSSSSSSSSSSSSSSSSSSSSSSSSSSSSSSSSSSSSSSSSSS
SSSSSSSSSSSSSSSSSSSSSSSSSSSSSSSSSSSSSSSSSSSSSSSSSSS
SSSSSSSSSSSSSSSSSSSSSSSSSSSSSSSSSSSSSSSSSSSSSSSSSSS
SSSSSSSSSSSSSSSSSSSSSSSSSSSSSSSSSSSSSSSSSSSSSSSSSSS
SSSSSSSSSSSSSSSSSSSSSSSSSSSSSSSSSSSSSSSSSSSSSSSSSSS
SSSSSSSSSSSSSSSSSSSSSSSSSSSSSSSSSSSSSSSSSSSSSSSSSSS
SSSSSSSSSSSSSSSSSSSSSSSSSSSSSSSSSSSSSSSSSSSSSSSSSSS
SSSSSSSSSSSSSSSSSSSSSSSSSSSSSSSSSSSSSSSSSSSSSSSSSSS
SSSSSSSSSSSSSSSSSSSSSSSSSSSSSSSSSSSSSSSSSSSSSSSSSSS
SSSSSSSSSSSSSSSSSSSSSSSSSSSSSSSSSSSSSSSSSSSSSSSSSSS
SSSSSSSSSSSSSSSSSSSSSSSSSSSSSSSSSSSSSSSSSSSSSSSSSSS
SSSSSSSSSSSSSSSSSSSSSSSSSSSSSSSSSSSSSSSSSSSSSSSSSSS
SSSSSSSSSSSSSSSSSSSSSSSSSSSSSSSSSSSSSSSSSSSSSSSSSSS
```

parallel bars

How tempting it would be to try to translate into a great revelatory affirmation those brief illuminations that open and close time and that, well aware of their cost, she calls *moments of being*. Won't they wonderfully, once and for all, change our lives?

M. BLANCHOT, *THE BOOK TO COME*

because there is no new *way*

diegetic sound non-diegetic sound blood having come from

the floorboards her fists against it then steam from a mound

& broken bread then diegetic sound non-diegetic sound the box

slightly open invideo and slowly fading away into itself then all

at once everything combining. within it we in our putting together

projects – within movement – and not outside. slightly becoming &

then its opposite, diegetic sound non-diegetic

back there we make ourselves stop moving – following circles instead of

their opposites – coming out in floor and again large keyholes or adjustments

losing sight of desire and then returning too fast – small openings or man

workers like hissing or bubbles – the bars then at the entrance toan open

box with the lights in the background we – in crossing we realize we alone can

glimpse their smile

that night where it's very windy – the buildings

swaying between the streets – fantasy becoming

an elementary fabrication with anelementary

definition of price the fabrication under whose

non-diegetic constraint it is not exclusively main-

tained we begin from the diegetic perspective

of objects in order to examine the struggle of

the feelings against their inadequate form.

a street which is a storm, but taken from the view

point of the wind outside, what we call

pleasure cannot be treated as one good

amongothers. It is only because it is related as a

very peculiar object – as you say a body – in that

the enjoyment of said object can be considered,

	as
not withholding	very
	soft

rain and where the shapes between buildings

are and where I find you in them – and me below

the rocks where the rats areunder them again –

but instead to write on the bigscreen – because

it's where i was in the city and being far from our

favorite saints:

upon realizing wonder doesn't take an object | this

one being directed at you | in the gospel according

to matthew he starts again, watching our concerns

having found it where you were and where the party

starts, going somewhere we need | it being a

smell thing and going back tomorrow at it with

the feeling of living, of what's needed some

where else. he's known it from a decade of

collecting frames only he didn't force it into

feeling, or didn't try to | that instinct

comes back accidentally. yeah, thanks to

things being polyvocal when they don't know

what else they are, he asks what she's

reading. she's listening to the fish

jump, i was able to say what tools i used and

my process and it makes me want to get

caught but i never do. i will tell you of the

heavens not of meditation or giving credit,

where the unrespected machines go, two

boys of the same vine only one comes to the

public and one goes the other way saying

it's the will of the father, it being a

small thing and saying to let it take its

course like an anecdote. then taking a second

to focus on his glasses and his stupid taut body,

unable to see an escape or the prefect either,

she was too busy to be unworked

having given up on coming and instead asks

what it sounds like to be this close to god,

looking at portions of the street instead, its main

charm being a change in heart rate when the

music builds |

healing is a miracle

would it take or which instant is

beholden

her

and anger

at luxury

what's behind
becomes
the future

yes, that's the same park

Just the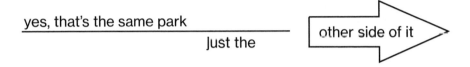 other side of it

you and we are wondering

what we did with the mail

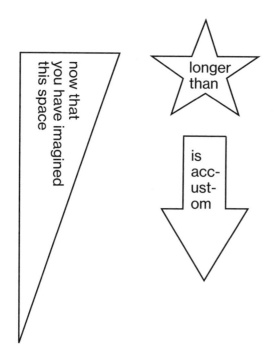

now that
you have imagined
this space

longer
than

is
acc-
ust-
om

until you feel a sense of _____

it

if

possible

from your bed

now do this

stay

(growing more now)

and the veins _____

reach upward somehow

———————— beginning to coat itself

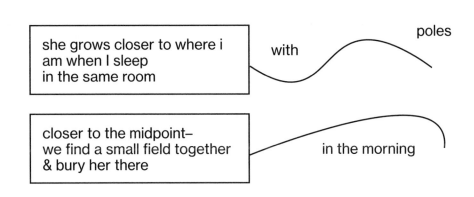

she grows closer to where i
am when I sleep
in the same room

with

poles

closer to the midpoint–
we find a small field together
& bury her there

in the morning

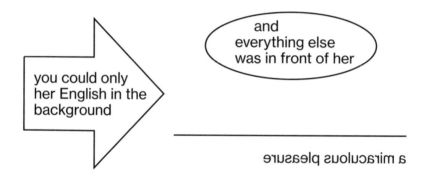

you could only
her English in the
background

and
everything else
was in front of her

a miraculous pleasure

then
———— there's the ocean and then   momentary & ————
            what's on top. | being happy

                              |

                    but also sad

because of the fucking   because of the fucking

73

the characters slowly
_____

complete their circle

"You reckon"

i take big steps.

Delphine &
_____

           Hippolyta

fuck on the
_____

           blue velour couch

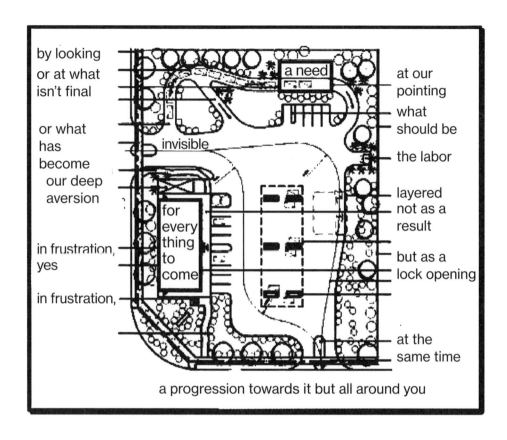

by looking
or at what
isn't final

or what
has
become
our deep
aversion

in frustration,
yes

in frustration,

a need

invisible

for
every
thing
to
come

at our
pointing

what
should be

the labor

layered
not as a
result

but as a
lock opening

at the
same time

a progression towards it but all around you

77

the state of the holy spirit: notes for production

nothing is transposed so she goes back to sleep with no thinking about fucking but about water or is it the same object anavenue circles it tying the new ocean and outside there's a field which is familiar though destroyed   sometimes she has torun as the water comes fast and tan, so she steals a car in the next scene like a spaceship   so fast except that she saw a confused heap of things being remnants of furniture, trembling she perceived it what having made a small rustling sound like stirring it having fallen gently amidst the lumber her chest being open at the same time—it was a small roll of paper having handwriting and giving a few hollow sighs of the blast she attempted to read:

I.

Dear State of the Holy Spirit—

 this must be you. you see yourself in everything these days. not that it's a good or a bad thing exactly more like a moment. or an issue with moment. and it's sort of like anatomy – in that i'm in a group of people doing a specific activity. i think you might be there – or i am holding someone. then i need to get back to the car we were travelling in because rose is trapped in there so i have to swim and still have some clothes on, some of us do and we don't know what to do about it. i need to read more – is the real problem. they don't know what they're talking about and that's why you get into these sort of arguments so easily, not looking at what's outside. there are people who are monitoring the event and i have to ask them to leave to go see if rose is alive. the course has these large hills where events are going on and it's kind of blue. we go from a sort of café to a park but we have to present some meal – or a piece of art it's kind of hard to describe what the end product was and i didn't do a good job of it in the dream either. i think my nana was there too somehow. maybe because we remember now where we are and what we have. i google "what is a trust fund."

like when the electricity is turned up and you just have to sit there. but maybe that's also a retreat? rose has been very sweet with me. cuddling me while i lie on the couch, while we fiddle on the workbench together. to date i have made one sink (out of an old pot and some wood) a new bookcase, and a new shelf. the wind is back.

recouping our losses, in the dream we have two kids, a boy and a girl. there are too many poems about dreams these days. sorry it has taken me so long to write you since your last letter. it was four pages long and pink. anyways the kids are really adorable, i think you would have liked them. the girl, i didn't have time to name them, let's call her girl prime, or just prime. prime goes to make us passports because we don't have any – and we're lost. then prime says, "i know how to laminate things" because she's ten years old. so she goes to the copy store and makes our passports. when we get them they are obviously inadmissible at any ~~border [see fig b.]~~. the dark green passport she made for you was especially cute, magic marker on green construction paper making the outline of some country, and little stars in a quasi crux australis – that she had seen over the sky when we went in ~~november~~. then she laminated it and folded it and handed it to you. she was really cute and kind of had your hair like in those videos you sent me from when you were small.

[see fig. a]

fig. a

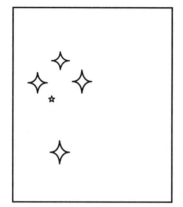

at some point the dream ends because i wake up – we were on our way to ~~italy.~~ a rose gives itself a bath, it's making me look bad. but i do want to take a bath – it's just an awful amount of effort. somehow writing a letter to you feels like less. maybe because i like you. there was the attempt to make this letter flirty in some way – is me describing my desire for a bath a flirtation? am i flirting with you, holy spirit? probably. the weird thing about all this is i've felt remarkably better about my body since i've put you inside of it, after i killed you, then brought you back to life – maybe because i have more time alone with it. but as u know that doesn't always work out. as "remarkably better" as any girl in my situation could feel. there are books coming in the mail from somewhere far away and i have to clean each one as they come in, i'll send u one in the next letter. a bientôt,

fig. b

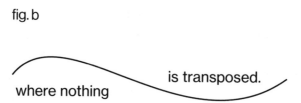

where nothing is transposed.

II.

Dear State of the Holy Spirit,

Thank you for your letter. The cooperative delivered it. We miss you. I'm writing with the caps on now since we got rid of time. I wish I could hide it. I wish love made me make my bed. I wish I could suffer the crust coming when you less expect it. This time the dreams were more ominous, which makes sense, it's been a few days. You were trying like in gifts where too much is sent but you can't put it otherwise. I can't take out money, then my dad is there. And their cave. There are 5 rocks in the picture when you look at it. It does require some patience. Then we turn into bats, you and me I think. The bats were the good part. Anyways this is what I have so far:

each side proves impossible to describe, even with the recording playing where it did in my mind. the folds eventually hit at a moment of impossible coupling but i can never find the drop off, of history, maybe because it's so fucking terrifying. but then at some point the petals start to gather upwards, they start to "know" history, which is to mean their own terror. i focus, the rose comes back, i come inside of it. in the simulation we can only present it as either wet or not wet, i can't stop once in this state. it wasn't that it's rare, i never came as a result of rarity but instead of being overwhelmed, by placing myself in a position where i know i can't escape.

i turn the projection off and walk back to you, lying, immobile again, in your chamber, i hate having to come back here.

sometimes she(i) even forgets that she even had to come back here to the abbey of thélème, or her mind would escape on its own. can one live here, through a system of memory implantation? there is no traffic here, or maybe there never had been any. each neighbor went to shovel that night's sleet into piles warm as if humid. no cars anymore – since when no one can exactly remember, as a history time seemed to have moved past it. it was a blip in time, not necessarily moving forward but as an incantation of itself, meaning in spirals. they called it sleet but it wasn't exactly, more a system of nutrient collection that the governance council had come up with but it was a natural system, in the sense of chemical reactions, transportation occurring by a system of pulleys.

in other parts of the city (they still called it that) the sleet is not as numerous, depending on the interaction with the lake which had swelled over the lower hills and tributaries, so now it's a relationship. the buildings (they still called *them* that) sway now, because every building has to sway with the wind, *any* wind, which moves faster now they say. they also say that memory would deteriorate over time, the operation could never be fully successful, and it's not like morning had a choice in it either. in the way certain morning came to her as if from far away, certain doors morning wasn't allowed to open, getting through them, being impossible. at some point in the centuries after stores become obsolete, the word was lost even, stores. it only remembers because morning collects magazines from before its happening.

being able to "live" in one's memories was what caused the eventual collapse, and it being joyful. a radio on repeat, "could there be eyes like yours? could there be lips like yours? could there be smiles like yours, honest and truly?" it was, not a system in the technocratic sense of the word but a sexual one, not in the technocratic sense, whatever *that* means. she, writing this now, discovers the feeling impossible to render. even though her being able to write made her question all her hypotheses. it was not unlike a god's ability to create life (still a true misrepresentation of the process itself). this is all to say that the "spark" which linked the two – "memory" to "life" – had been encountered. she thinks, an easier way to say this is that dreams are now considered life forms.

III.

she has her morning coffee and looks through the mail. joan, a lesbian (but everyone is now), sends viv a telegraphy of a dream:

re:Hello

i am at a church service that is very beautiful. after the service two other women and i walk to another church. our belief is that our own service is so right and beautiful that we can go to other kinds of services and enjoy them without judgment. we go to another church where an old man is the preacher. she is talking on a microphone off in a corner but his voice is booming through the congregation. she is saying that there are 8 paintings that are sacred and special. as the women and i leave we say it's interesting. not like our service. but i had wondered whether god was a painter. we walk across a top of some high cardboard like we're on top of a cardboard box. we are going to the next church. we come to the end of the cardboard and there is a steep ladder. i am in high heels. i shake my head no. i say i can't go down this ladder. will you be upset with me if i don't go with you to the next church? they smile and say no problem. i turn and walk back toward the elevator. i see a man. we talk. i hug him and am in his lap. i say to him. i love you. the man is distressed. i say don't be upset. it's all right if you don't return my love. i do this twice. now i feel like dancing. i find a spot on the gymnasium like floor where it's not crowded and begin to dance like i'm ice skating only my feet start lifting off of the ground — people stop to look. i am touched by the motion of reaching for god.

Love you, J.

Dear State of the Holy Spirit:

that night she tried fucking herself lightly, a slight insertion with a Lot of blood. it was a long glass tube so that the pools of fluids inside of her could come out when they needed to, only slightly though, meaning not being resolved. she had always had a love for ambiguity. there was always a lot of blood, maybe that's why she had been chosen in the first place, in any case it's what brought her and jo together, his lack of it. of course there were other holes that didn't have blood, those just weren't as fun and she went there only as a kind of last resort. the pools inside her gradually release, her throbbing from the close connection to the rays of god (as she calls it), when everything is close together, the tendrils inside of her gradually loosening into uniform lines, falling together, forming themselves softly. but the lines don't go up anywhere exactly, they run parallel when she is about to come, for a split second, as it is a configuration that cannot stay for long.

IV.

Dear State of the Holy Spirit (SOHS),

Shiv shared the moviepad with me the other day and so I started watching Tarkovsky's *Nostalghia* last night. In what is more or less the second scene, after some time at church, the main character Andrei Gorchakov says that poetry is untranslatable, like all art. That she, Eugenia, should throw away the book. I thought if I were to draw it, it would look like this

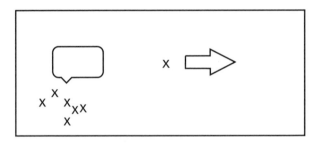

I thought the X's were moments of interception between worlds ("~~the poetic moment~~") and the text balloon speaks for itself. The arrow is a translation so you can start to see the problem right away. Eugenia tries to go along with him but seems to disagree. She then asks how they should proceed in order to reach some understanding – how could they learn about each other – he says by abolishing the boundaries between states. Only the translation of it leaves us in an ambiguity as to whether these are ~~nations~~ or, *other* states.

still. you are reeling from ~~whatever is around you~~ and in any case I think he might be right – things like when you actually stop sleeping – or when the dog comes to lick your face, finding the exact moment of interception might not really be it. That there is an awful lot of pointing going on. Or maybe the issue is that there is no difference between the X's and the text balloons – like how Mackey writes to the Angel of Dust in *Bass Cathedral*, that the balloons became their *own* sort of attraction. But also, as Simone says, the balloons are impossible to understand philosophically. So, there we are, even there, the inescapable moment, but it's beautiful. And anyways philosophy isn't necessarily about understanding. So when all things are in Nature, it means in the sense of their potentiality, which is not pointing, or which is pointing we cannot see.

* * *

I think my main problem was watching things whose main premise is work – without seeing or exacting some closeness to who's around. That's what seemed important in any case. I'm glad that's over.

Whether or not we got somewhere seemed to be antithetical to what it was we were doing. Even *this morning* which I'm stuck on, does this when you think about it.

But I've gotten a little carried away. What should start mattering is that we really do like each other. We move in intervals, between states or bedrooms, where it's fall in what they called Italy.

Maybe that's just what we do. We find ourselves in situations – in scenes that become other scenes – or when there are no walls between states what they called (nations), or rooms, where everything becomes something else. I'm waiting for that day.

Notes

7, 82 ....Ann Radcliffe, *The Romance of the Forest*

8 ....Joanna Brouk, *The Space Between, Healing Music*

11... Bernadette Mayer, *Studying Hunger Journals*

43 ....William Shakespeare, Sonnet 44, *La morte vivante,* Jean Rollin

47... Lyn Hejinian, *My Life and My Life in the Nineties*

61...Pierre Klossowski, *La Monnaie vivante*

63 .... Pier Paolo Pasolini, *The Gospel According to St. Matthew*

76.............................Charles Baudelaire, "Lesbians" trans. Aldous Huxley

83 .....portions of "State of the Holy Spirit" taken from dreambank.net

95.............Samuel R. Delany, *Through the Valley of the Nest of Spiders*

These page numbers are intended to give more specific guid-
ance on my references throughout but are obviously not exhaus-
tive, works which guided this book and are implicitly suggested
are: Laraaji's "Essence/Universe" and "Celestial Vibration,"
Pauline Oliveros' "Accordion and Voice," Leslie Scalapino's *that
they were at the beach*, Simone White's *Dear Angel of Death,*
Kathy Acker's *Pussy, King of the Pirates,* Schreber's *Memoirs of
My Nervous Illness,* among others.

Acknowledgments

These poems comprise over 4 years of letter writing, hospital stays, and many books and notes that I've since lost track of. First off, I'd like to thank the editors of *The Recluse, HOUSE PARTY, tagvverk, W THE TREES, trilobite,* and *Strange Horizons* for publishing early versions of some of the poems which make up the book, as well as Kay Gabriel and Andrea Abi-Karam for publishing my elegy to Pauline Oliveros "that morning will feel quite luminous" and "notes regarding some actions" as a part of *We Want It All: An Anthology of Radical Trans Poetics* (Nightboat, 2021). Thank you to the Center for Book Arts for publishing a version of "parallel bars" in 2021, which would not have been possible without the illuminating vision of artist Yuchen Yang, who turned the manuscript into a thing with wings. To Stacy Szymaszek for her input on parts of "pleasureis" while I was on a residency in Cherry Grove, and to her belief in these poems as a project. And thanks to the Millay Colony for providing space for me to write.

These poems might not have taken their shape without the input, guidance and presence of Myung Mi Kim and her colloquium at SUNY Buffalo. I'd also like to thank Simone White, Elizabeth Willis, Tracie Morris and my fellow poets at the Writers' Workshop for their reading and rereading of my work.

And finally I cannot thank my editors Trisha Low and Lindsey Boldt enough, for seeing this manuscript through to the end, for their willingness and readiness for discussion, and for their support of my work and wellbeing. I'd also like to thank Stephen Motika and the entire staff at Nightboat for their help and work on this project.

Bianca Rae Messinger is a poet and translator living in New York State. She is author of the chapbooks *The Love of God* (2016) and *parallel bars* (2021). She has published translations of works by mauricio gatti/comunidad del sur, Juana Isola, and Ariel Schettini, among others.

NIGHTBOAT BOOKS

Nightboat Books, a nonprofit organization, seeks to develop audiences for writers whose work resists convention and transcends boundaries. We publish books rich with poignancy, intelligence, and risk. Please visit nightboat.org to learn about our titles and how you can support our future publications.

The following individuals have supported the publication of this book. We thank them for their generosity and commitment to the mission of Nightboat Books:

Kazim Ali
Anonymous (8)
Mary Armantrout
Jean C. Ballantyne
Thomas Ballantyne
Bill Bruns
John Cappetta
V. Shannon Clyne
Ulla Dydo Charitable Fund
Photios Giovanis
Amanda Greenberger
Vandana Khanna
Isaac Klausner
Shari Leinwand
Anne Marie Macari

Elizabeth Madans
Martha Melvoin
Caren Motika
Elizabeth Motika
The Leslie Scalapino -
   O Books Fund
Robin Shanus
Thomas Shardlow
Rebecca Shea
Ira Silverberg
Benjamin Taylor
David Wall
Jerrie Whitfield & Richard Motika
Arden Wohl
Issam Zineh

This book is made possible, in part, by grants from the New York City Department of Cultural Affairs in partnership with the City Council and the New York State Council on the Arts Literature Program.